I is for Idols

Dr. C. White-Elliott

www.clfpublishing.org
909.315.3161

Cover Design by Senir Design: sd_grpx01@yahoo.com

ISBN # 978-1-945102-60-8

Printed in the United States of America.

For

Mister Williams

The first of the Ten Commandments says, *"I am the* LORD *your God, who brought you out of Egypt, out of the land of slavery. You shall have no other gods before me."*

(Exodus 20:2-3)

Sometimes without even realizing it, we give more attention to things or people in our life than we do to God. When we do that, we make those items or people mini gods. They become idols to us, stealing our attention away from God.

Keep in mind that although God wants us to have nice things and to live an enjoyable life, He does not want anything to replace our love for Him.

One thing that people idolize is their cars. They spend a lot of time and money on their cars.

No matter how nice looking a car is or how much fun you can have with it, a car should not get more of your attention than God does.

Video games and other electronics take up a lot of people's time and attention, and many people use technology for school and jobs.

Technology has become very important in our life, but like everything else technology has its place.

Do not allow your use of video games, cell phones, and computers distract you from worshipping God.

When technology fails, God will still be here for you.

Many children and young adults are blinded by the stardom of their favorite entertainers. Every time the person puts out a new song or video, their fans run to the computer to download or watch it.

It's okay to be someone's fan or to have role models, but that person's life and words should not dictate your life.

Your life must follow the words of God in the Bible.

Remember, go to church with your family or a neighbor and read your Bible.

Fashion has become very popular in this day and age.

Every few months or so, there is a new fashion craze, whether it's new sneakers, a new logo, a new hairstyle, or the new color of the season.

And, everyone has to have them.

There is nothing wrong with wanting to look your best.

But, you must not allow fashion to consume you and take God's place in your life.

Money is very important in the world and in every day life. Without money, we will not be able to do the things we need to, such as buy food, clothes, personal items or pay our bills.

We must remember that the Bible says, *"For the **love** of money is the root of all of evil"* (1 Timothy 6:10).

So, we should not be chasing after money, and we should not allow money to take our focus off the most important love we have in our life: the love we have for God.

God will supply our every need. We just need to keep our focus and attention on Him.

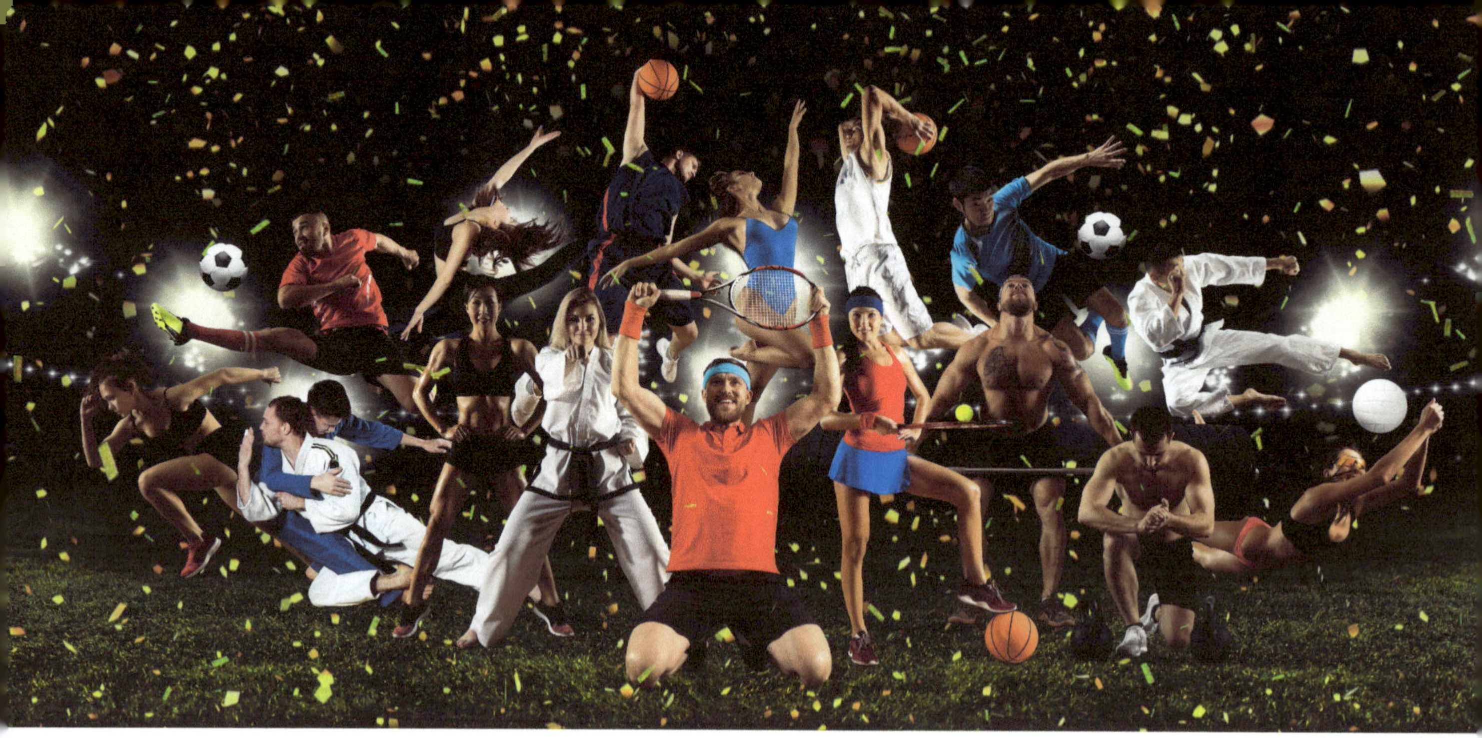

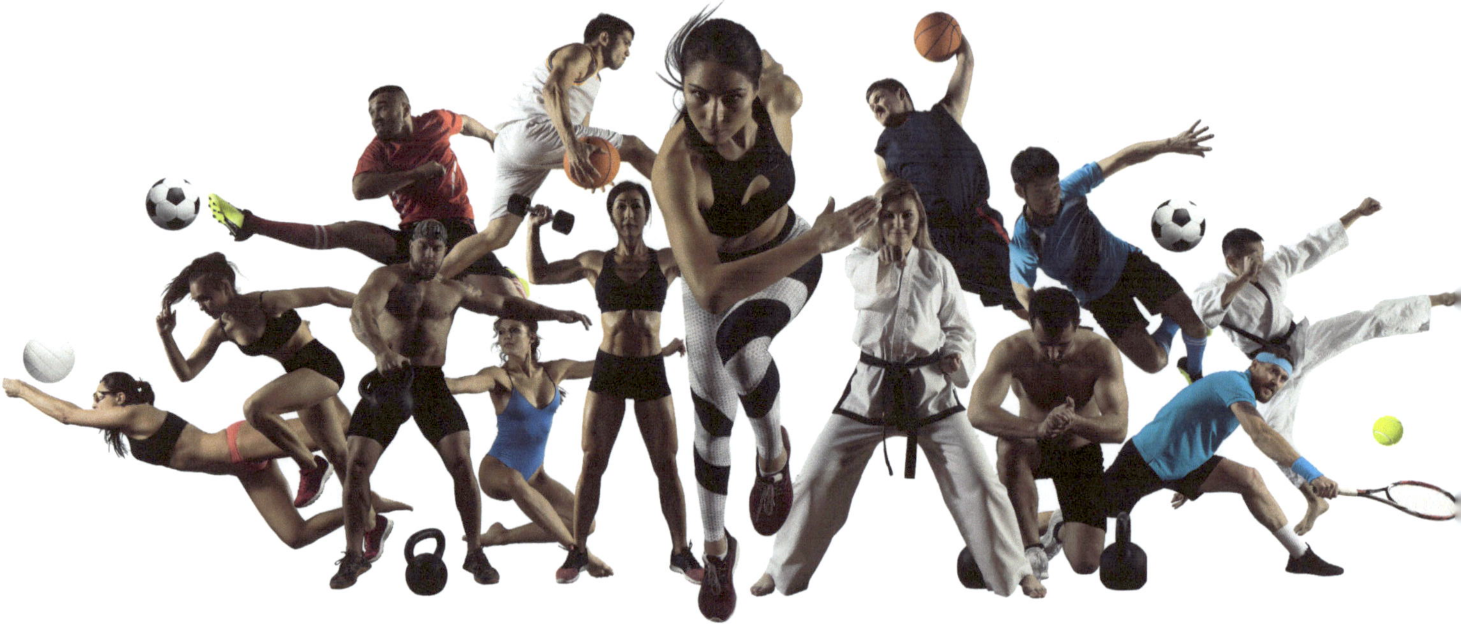

Many people love sports. They either play sports themselves, used to play sports, watch them on television,
or all of the above.

Sports help people make friends, help them exercise and stay in good shape and be healthy, and it teaches them many skills.

Sports become unhealthy when all people want to do is play or watch sports and it keeps them from going to church or studying their Bible.

In the Bible, Jesus said He came to give us life

and life more abundant.

But, that does not mean all the things we have

in life should blind us and become mini gods,

trying to take the place of God.

God must be first in our lives.

Nothing should ever take His place.

www.ingramcontent.com/pod-product-compliance
Lightning Source LLC
Chambersburg PA
CBHW041956100426
42813CB00019B/2903